101
REASONS
to be
EPISCOPALIAN

101 REASONS to be EPISCOPALIAN

Compiled by Louie Crew

MOREHOUSE PUBLISHING
A Continuum imprint
HARRISBURG • LONDON • NEW YORK

101 reasons to be Episcopalian / compiled by Louie Crew.
    p. cm.
    ISBN 0-8192-1925-8 (pbk.)
    1. Episcopal Church—Doctrines.
I. Title: One hundred and one reasons to be Episcopalian.
II. Title: One hundred one reasons to be Episcopalian.
III. Crew, Louie, 1936–
    BX5930.3 .A13 2003
    283'.73—dc21

                                    2002153013

Foreword

We Episcopalians are a merry lot. Not humble . . .
God knows, never humble. But almost always
merry and almost always self-deprecating. In
fact, in all the Lord God's panoply of Christian
families, none parodies itself and its own
peculiarities more than we do.

As a young woman, I used to wonder about
the why of our constant jesting even as I too
was reveling in all the old, tired jokes and trying to discover new ones to add to my own
cache of them. . . . Whiskopalians; God's most
literate communion; Romans on birth control;
Smells and their cousins, the Bells; the daven-
ning Christians . . . I knew them all and I
employed them all—wherein, I have finally
realized, lies the key.

I "employed" them in my young adulthood,
as I still "employ" them in maturity, because
without them I could not engage the beauty of
the thing and survive. That awful holiness of
God in human space would suck me into its
center and fix me there; and I would become,
like a wick intoxicated with the fire, consumed
before the night had ended. But by means of
humor when I am at large in the world, and

through the use of symbols and rituals, icons and arcane lexicon when I am among my own kind, I manage to co-habit joyfully with what I can not bear to articulate directly.

It is the poetry of faith, not its various dogma, that persuades us Episcopalians. The elegance of a doctrine . . . the music of a holy name . . . the cry of the eagle in the chant of a psalm. . . . These things teach us, though most of them can not themselves be taught. They are the aura of God and the truth of Christ beyond all telling, but firmly within our worship. And while each of them can be named, none of them can be described any more than can "Paraclete" or sanctus or the regularly-scheduled heartbreak of fraction.

As a result, we come together, we Episcopalians, as a body of men and women disturbed by beauty and made absurd by the passion of an holy aesthetic. We find each other by affinity and wish only that we could reach out to all others like us; but lacking the language of such discourse, we don't quite know how. So we joke to declare ourselves as part of the public conversation. We joke and hope to make of our humor a kind of mating call for those whom we seek to attract as kinsmen.

This book is not itself a collection of jokes, though there are many references to them here. Nor is this a book of Episcopalian patois speaking itself in the language of symbols and Latinate phrasings. Nor do I mean to suggest that every Episcopalian will agree with everything said here. Such as that would never happen with this or any other book, for we are also a contrary lot in our faithfulness. Rather and wonderfully, this is just a little book of confession, and nothing more. That is, this small volume is as near, probably, as most Episcopalians can get to naming the affinities that are the familial markings of our part of God's family. It is also, perhaps most poignantly, in fact, a merry attempt not only to name our sensibilities to one another but also to reveal our ways as best we can to those others whose company we so yearn for. May God bless these words of ours to the use of both those endeavors.

Phyllis Tickle
The Farm in Lucy

The Feast of St. Francis
of Assisi, 2002

Introduction

I'm delighted that you're reading this little
book. It has saving news about the Episcopal
Church in it, news that Episcopalians too
often keep secret—not because we want to
exclude you, but because we believe that it's
the Holy Spirit's job to persuade. Our job is to
welcome you and be a friend. Yet we become
almost ecstatic when we tell what we like
about the Episcopal Church. You'll see that as
you read through the entries in this book. If
you're already an Episcopalian, I hope that
you'll let this little book prompt you to be an
evangelist in ways that are specifically
Episcopal. You have good news to tell. Feel
free to tell it enthusiastically!

This book includes 101 of the best reasons
from a collection on my web site of 365+ reasons for being Anglican/Episcopalian. Take
some of your own favorites and add to them.
Put this book on a table in your living room or
in the break room at work. It will probably
generate lots of curiosity and conversation.

Ask friends at your parish to tell you about
their reasons for being Episcopalian. Put their
answers in a fancy format and post them in

the parish hall, or mail them out with your newsletter. You'll end up with a wildly varied collection, but each of you will discover one truth: Episcopalians are a thinking lot, and where there are two of us, there will be at least two opinions, if not more. Each of us has a different reason to be Episcopalian—and each reason is equally valid.

In Confessional churches, people expend much energy trying to agree on one clear set of answers to life's questions. Not so with most Episcopalians. Most of us wouldn't want to be in a denomination that pretends to have all the answers, or where people are never allowed to disagree. We value our right to disagree and remain in the same Communion.

And we've been that way right from the start. We're not a confessional church. From our beginnings in Elizabethan England and in the American colonies, Anglicans and Episcopalians have rarely had enough members to afford the luxury of requiring everyone to think alike—some persons in this little book take theological positions radically different from the positions of others in this book. But we all come to the same Table, and in these statements we suggest why.

We come to the Table because the Episcopal Church is a place where God loves us before we decide whether we love God. We come because here it is safe to doubt, because no one will force us to claim a certainty we don't feel. Most of us can probably say the Creed without setting off a lie detector, but we rejoice that the Episcopal Church doesn't require one.

Do we care about belief? Yes, passionately. Do we care about God and Jesus? Yes, passionately. But we know that we don't have a corner on the truth. We know that we don't have priority access to God and Jesus. We can look back on our long history with some embarrassment about times when our church was wrong about slavery, colonialism, and the role of women. But looking at the same history we can also see God leading us to repentance and to a renewed commitment to justice.

God forgives us all our sins. In the Episcopal Church, we don't have to harbor and dwell on our sins continually. That's why we have an altar. We leave our sins there. In the Eucharist God makes us all blood kin. We pray to be forgiven as we forgive. We don't get rid of our enemies; we learn to love them instead.

And there are a lot of us. The Episcopal Church has over 7,200 congregations, in 108 dioceses, eight of them outside the domestic USA. We have one of the most democratic forms of governance in Christendom. Bishops and priests don't hold all the power. Definitive opinions aren't handed down from on high. Lay and clergy share authority equally in our House of Deputies at General Convention, and neither The House of Bishops nor The House of Deputies can establish official policy for the Episcopal Church without the approval of the other. In fact, most policy is set at the diocesan level. My bishop likes to describe our diocese as one church with 120 mission stations. Episcopal congregations share resources; we undertake tasks together that we couldn't even consider were each congregation to do the task alone. We hold ourselves accountable in stewardship not just to ourselves, but to the community, the diocese, and to the common mission of the Episcopal Church nationally and beyond.

But we're not the same as we used to be. Several stereotypes regarding Episcopalians reveal less than they did years ago. Few view us as 'the Republican Party at Prayer' these days. We're much more catholic than we once were, and we no longer rent our pews based on class and other markers of privilege. Still, we sustain a higher regard for tradition and form than do many Protestant groups. Witness this in the jokes we tell about ourselves:

"How many Episcopalians does it take to put in a light bulb?" the wag asks. "Three," he tells us: "One to put in the light bulb; one to make the martinis; another to talk about how much prettier the old light bulb was."

Or this joke: St. Peter greets new arrivals trying to enter heaven, each from a different religious group. He turns down the Jew because, "You ate pork." He turns down the Baptist because "That was wine, not grape juice that you drank." He turns down the Episcopalian because, "You used the wrong salad fork."

Episcopalians believe that God made the ticklebox, and it's our responsibility to keep it in good repair, so we laugh generously at ourselves. We try not to take ourselves too seriously.

But we're serious about some things: I keep all my diplomas and awards in the closet, but I have always kept on my wall the framed certificate of my confirmation at St. Peter's in

Rome, Georgia on October 29, 1961 at the age of 24. Few choices in my life have so shaped me or so enriched me as that one did. I've met Jesus in the Episcopal Church time after time, and at the end of the encounter, Jesus always sends me out into the world in peace, to do the work that God wants me to do, rejoicing in the power of the Holy Spirit.

And ultimately, that's what it's all about. We're not proud of ourselves, but of God and of the good news. And we think you will be too. We invite you to let us see God in your countenance among us.

Louie Crew

101
REASONS

1

"[W]hen Anglicanism is at its best, its liturgy, its poetry, its music and its life can create a world of wonder in which it is very easy to fall in love with God."

Urban T. Holmes, III

2 From smells and bells to speaking in tongues—we have it all.

Sheena A. Lawrence
Diocese of Atlanta

3

I became an Episcopalian because of an invitation in a Sunday bulletin: "All baptized Christians are welcome at the Lord's Table." The state of my life, my marriage, my lostness didn't matter. I responded to a community's magnanimity of spirit. Through them I learned of God's abiding love affair with us through the Risen Christ in whom we live and move and have our being.

The Rev. Jessica A. Hatch
Diocese of Utah

4

"We have a faith not afraid to reason and reason not ashamed to adore."
—The Late Rt. Rev. Daniel Sylvester Tuttle

The Rev. W. Lee Shaw
Diocese of Utah

5

The seasons are color coded.

Bungee Bynum
Diocese of Lexington

6

The Episcopal Church enables me to worship God with my mind. It doesn't install an idol like the Bible or the Pope as the source of ultimate authority. It has lived in the tension between ancient truth and living history and has evolved into something fragile but beautiful, something that is worthy of being defended as it becomes a sign of the inclusive Kingdom of God.

The Rt. Rev. John S. Spong
Diocese of Newark

7

Episcopalians see reality as existing in the tensions of paradox, ambiguity, and diversity.

Richard C. Milhon
Diocese of Kansas

8

I'm glad to be a member of the Episcopal Church because it's evangelical, catholic, pentecostal, and liberal. It is evangelical because it glories in the cross of Jesus Christ as salvation for all people. It's catholic in that it is a church that lives as resurrection people beyond the blight and bondage of death. We're pentecostal because we trust in the supernatural empowerment of the Holy Spirit. And we're liberal because we yearn for the Kingdom of God in the world as it is in heaven and labor in the hope that will make it so.

Bishop Alden Hathaway
Pittsburgh, retired
Diocese of Florida

9

Anglicans do good deeds to increase understanding of God, not out of fear or to earn admission to heaven.

Robert L. Neal III
Diocese of Chicago

10

Asking questions about our faith is expected. In the Episcopal Church, God doesn't get upset if I wonder why some things are as they are. And God doesn't get upset if I suggest that some things should not continue as they are.

La Reverenda
Martha Sylvia Ovalle Vasquez
Diocese of Delaware

At our best, Episcopalians can respectfully disagree about a great many things—and still break bread together.

Barbara Tensen Ross
Diocese or Oregon

12

I'm an Episcopalian because of the incredibly profound understanding of authority in the Anglican Communion. The three-legged stool—with its stout legs of Scripture, tradition, and reason, supported by (but also firmly joined by) the seat of our experience and prayer—is perhaps Anglicanism's most glorious contribution to theology.

Paul M. Johns
Diocese of Olympia

13

We believe that love without justice is cheap sentimentality.

Carter Heyward
Diocese of Massachusetts

14

My four-year-old son has attended the Episcopal Church since birth. He sings the Alleluia from the fraction anthem as easily as the theme from "Blue's Clues."

The Rev. Rachel Endicott
Diocese of Olympia

15

When asked if he was saved, Archbishop of Canterbury William Temple replied, "I have been saved, I am being saved, I hope to be saved." That understanding of faith, hope, and humility reinforces me as an Episcopalian/Anglican.

Dean George L. W. Werner
Diocese of Pittsburgh

16

We do not give simple answers to complex questions. Instead, we offer tools that help people develop a sustaining faith.

B. Lance Moody
Diocese of Oklahoma

17

My mind is Protestant and my spirit is liturgical. Where other than to the Book of Common Prayer can my worship go and still have both be happy?

> *Phyllis Tickle*
> *Diocese of West Tennessee*

18

Ours is not just a checkbook ministry.
Episcopalians roll up their sleeves and help.

Agnes L. Haviland-Moore
Diocese of Connecticut

19

We have full-bodied worship: bow, kneel, sit, stand, kneel, hug, walk, and sometimes even raise your hands, cry, laugh, sing, shout, whisper, smell, taste, feel, touch, hold, see, and behold and on and on.

The Very Rev. Marilyn J. Engstrom
Diocese of Wyoming

20

Where the road to Easter is never a short cut, but you always get there.

The Rev. Dr. Barbara T. Cheney
Diocese of Connecticut

21
Pregnant priests! Celebrating!

The Rev. Deborah Galante Seles
Diocese of Chicago

I love Anglicanism for its basic humanity, its sense of decency and order, its freedom of thought and its insistence on the corpus of faith, "those things necessary unto salvation." I love it for its tradition and for the women and men of faith who have been lights of the generations in whose company we worship. I love it for its quirkiness, its untidiness, its comprehensiveness and for its ability to receive, accept, alter or jettison new things, while being always merely and astoundingly the Church.

Father Tony Clavier
Diocese of South Dakota

23

It's a church where you can come in without leaving your brain at the door and then have the opportunity to love all of those who managed to come in with their "wrong" ideas.

The Rt. Rev. Leo Frade, D.D.
Diocese of Southeast Florida

24

We belong before we believe.

Joanna Wragg
Diocese of Southeast Florida

25

Where faith is God's gift to us, not our gift
to God.

Louie Crew
Diocese of Newark

Like Catholic and Orthodox Christians, Episcopalians are in touch with the ancient voices and aesthetic and spiritual practices of the Christian tradition. We are united by a common liturgy and by the Book of Common Prayer. And so long as we do the liturgy right, we are orthodox, and thus permitted a broad range of theological opinions. With its riches of liturgy, prayer, and music, it is for me a sacrament of the sacred, and it feels like home.

Marcus J. Borg
Diocese of Oregon

27

No matter where in the world I attend an
Episcopal/Anglican church, I am always home.

Joan Carr
Diocese of British Columbia

28

We have the liturgical beauty of the Catholics combined with the local authority of the Southern Baptists.

Cynthia McLeod
Diocese of East Tennessee

29

The signs that say, "The Episcopal Church Welcomes You" mean it.

Nick Humez
Diocese of Newark

30

The Episcopal Church is a place where bishops are people too, and some of them know it. Many even have spouses to remind them.

Linda M. Maloney
Diocese of Minnesota

The Book of Common Prayer allows a degree of uniformity in prayer while leaving room for the diversity of cultures, languages and liturgical styles.

The Very Rev. David G. Bollinger
Diocese of Central New York

32

The Episcopal Church taught me that Jesus came to challenge, not just comfort; to overturn, not maintain; to love, not judge; to include, not cast aside.

The Rev. Canon Elizabeth R. Geitz
Diocese of New Jersey

33

Episcopalians try to love with the heart of Christ, think with the mind of Christ, and act as if we were the body of Christ.

Prof. Willis H. A. Moore
Diocese of Hawaii

34

I spent Good Friday with the folks at St. Paul's Chapel. There I talked with a young firefighter who has been volunteering at Ground Zero for several months. In the midst of his sharing he said: "If it weren't for this place, I wouldn't be able to smile."

Sharon Moon
Diocese of Washington

35

Because it's one religion where laughing at our own absurdities is a basic spiritual discipline and we're invited to rejoice in how much we have still to learn of God instead of how much we know.

L .William Countryman
Diocese of California

36

I love Anglicanism because the most stable seat, on rough ground, is a three-legged stool.

The Rev. Selwyn Swift
St. Edmundsbury and
Ipswich, Suffolk, England

37

Our eighth Sacrament: Fellowship and Good Food.

Amada Demers
Diocese of Texas

38

Our theology is an art form, not a law book.

Paul Gibson
Diocese of Toronto

39

From Miami to Manchester, from Lima to London, from Brisbane to Birmingham, Singapore to San Francisco, I can go to church and fit right in.

John F. Schwaller
Diocese of Minnesota

40

I am an Episcopalian because it is the one
form of the tradition that enables me to still
call myself a Christian. It allows me to think
and to feel deeply in a life that is grounded in
tradition and yet is always open to change. I
sometimes think of Anglicanism as the Zen
Buddhism of the West. I love it because
schism is a greater sin than heresy. I would
much rather be with someone who loved me
than with someone who could define love.

Alan Jones
Diocese of California

41

Where else can you be considered a "young person" until you are 40 years old?

Lesley M. Adams
Diocese of Rochester

42

We honor tradition but do not fossilize it.

Lee Canipe
Diocese of Virginia

43

We welcome the faithful, the seeker, and the doubter.

Diana Smith
Diocese of Washington

44

We promise to welcome you in Christ's name. We will honor the gifts you bring. We will invite you into our community, or wish you well if you choose another path.

Dorothy Isabel Crocker
Huron, Canada

45

We celebrate a Christmas Season and not just a Christmas Day.

The Rt. Rev. Jack M. McKelvey
Diocese of Rochester

46

Where God's unconditional love for all of us is celebrated every day.

Sen. Marge Kilkelly
Diocese of Maine

47

In the Episcopal Church doubt is so okay that
we name some parishes "St. Thomas."

Louie Crew
Diocese of Newark

48

Being an intelligent, strong woman is not a drawback in the Episcopal Church.

Cynthia Jo Mahaffey
Diocese of Ohio

Episcopalians may spend a lot of time arguing with each other about important matters inside and outside the church. And often the arguments are very public. Sometimes they go on for years and seem to reach no definite resolution. But Episcopalians are confident that in and through this kind of engagement with each other, they will come closer to understanding what God is up to and who God wants them, as a church, to be.

Ellen K. Wondra
Diocese of Rochester

50

As an Anglican I can be myself. I can be authentic and feel accepted and respected.

Glauco Soares de Lima
Bishop Primate of Brazil

51

Where the priesthood of all believers has a goodly chance of including everyone, including people of all shapes, sizes, ages, colors, and abilities.

The Rev. Dr. Barbara T. Cheney
Diocese of Connecticut

52

This is the only church that is as lovingly loony as your family.

Mary L. Lyons
Diocese of Olympia

53

Prayer that is time tested.

Cynthia McLeod
Diocese of East Tennessee

54

Tired of hell fire and brimstone? Try incense.

Louie Crew
Diocese of Newark

Another reason to be Episcopalian is that the altar is not fenced. In my days as a Presbyterian "seeker" I frequently attended both Roman Catholic and Episcopal liturgies: at the former I was explicitly refused communion; at the latter I was welcome to receive. As Woody Allen didn't quite say, I wouldn't want to belong to a club that wouldn't take me as a non-member.

Deborah Smith Douglas
Diocese of The Rio Grande

56

I like being an Episcopalian because I can be a mystic without anybody noticing.

Suzanne Guthrie
Diocese of New York

57

Anglicans can imagine the past and remember the future.

The Rev. Nayan McNeill, Ph.D.
Diocese of El Camino Real

58

We proudly wear ribbons of so many different colors.

Mary Jane Herron
Diocese of Newark

59

Two millennia of faith; four centuries of
liturgy; comrades worldwide traveling in love
the journey to God we each tread alone.

Peter Berry
Diocese of Bristol, England

60

The hymn: "One was a doctor and one was a queen and one was a shepherdess on the green and one was a soldier and one was a priest and one was slain by a fierce wild beast."

The Very Rev. Marilyn J. Engstrom
Diocese of Wyoming

61

Mystery and clarity co-exist here.

Alex H. MacDonell
Diocese of New Jersey

Despite or perhaps even precisely because of our present disagreements in the Episcopal Church I am reminded that God calls us all together because we aren't whole without each other.

Nancy A. G. Vogele
Diocese of Vermont

My favorite reason for being an Episcopalian is the coherence of scripture, tradition and reason/experience as basic tenets of our belief. I appreciate our melding of church and world, sacred and secular, soul and body, sophistication and simplicity, literary and non-verbal, seriousness and nonchalance, holiness and ordinariness, indeed, our being deeply rooted in the Incarnation.

The Rev. Malcolm Boyd
Diocese of Los Angeles

64

God loves you, and there's not a thing you can do to change that.

The Rev. Tom Van Culin
Diocese of Hawaii

65

We find our unity in shared worship, not in enforced agreement.

Lou Poulain
Diocese of El Camino Real

66

We leave neither our minds, nor our hearts, nor our bodies at the church door.

Larry Graham
Diocese of Atlanta

67

Episcopalians believe in moderation in all things, including moderation.

Sheena A. Lawrence
Diocese of Atlanta

68

I love our church because we don't think unity means uniformity.

Barbara Cawthorne Crafton
Diocese of New York

69

Hooker's Eucharistic theology in 30 seconds:
It's about us becoming the Body of Christ, the
presence of Christ in the assembled community.
For real.

The Rev. Deborah Galante Seles
Diocese of Chicago

70

In the Episcopal Church you will be treated as an adult, and the child in you will be welcomed.

Alex H. MacDonell
Diocese of New Jersey

71

Our roots in the past bear fruit in the present.

Alice Haugen
Diocese of Iowa

72

Christ has no hands on earth but ours. We need you to help us bless the world.

Meg Carter
Diocese of California

73

I am so appreciative of the way the Episcopal Church, with its Benedictine roots, keeps me grounded in real life, real relationships, real encounters. Ours is a very incarnational church—insisting on the importance of the Spirit's embodiment in the ordinary events of each day, and reminding us over and over that God can be found in the most difficult and improbable places.

Norvene Vest
Diocese of Los Angeles

Jesus said 'Feed my sheep,' but he didn't specify that they be fed a narrow and rigid diet. Our Episcopal/Anglican approach to the sacrament of Penance is a good example: 'All may, some should, none must.'

Dean George L. W. Werner
Diocese of Pittsburgh

In a global family, like the Anglican
Communion, the voice of prayer is never silent.

Canon James Rosenthal
Diocese of Canterbury
Canterbury, England

76

Women can be pastors and ministers, but only in the Episcopal church can they be priests.

Donna H. Barthle
Diocese of Central Pennsylvania

77

Though you pray without ceasing, you won't be called devout.

The Rev. Canon Bill Lewellis
Diocese of Bethlehem

78

One of the perks of membership in our parish is the exercise. My heart rate elevates with all the standing, kneeling, processing, bowing, passing the peace, reciting, crossing one's self and singing. Fortunately there is some time for a pulse check during the sermon and readings.

Lu Sweeney
Diocese of California

79

We eat, drink, and are merry, for we live in the Kingdom of our Lord Christ.

Ken Guthrie
Diocese of Alabama

80

We don't quiz you on your beliefs before worshipping with you.

James Handsfield
Diocese of Atlanta

81

Catholic lite. Great rite. Less guilt.

William Barnett-Lewis
Diocese of Milwaukee

82

The Prayer Book bids us to come to God's table for strength and renewal, not for solace and pardon only.

Agnes L. Haviland-Moore
Diocese of Connecticut

When you count acolytes, Chalice bearers, ushers, greeters, nursery people, altar guild, choir, and so on, there are more people involved in an Episcopal service than in any other. And there are more opportunities to be involved.

Donna H. Barthle
Diocese of Central Pennsylvania

84

I love our church because we have poetry in
our Prayer Book and in our Hymnal.

Barbara Cawthorne Crafton
Diocese of New York

85

My Jewish mother and Roman Catholic father found themselves welcomed into the Episcopal Church over fifty years ago as they sought a home for their young family. I grew up in the Episcopal Church feeling that everyone was welcome. My father, a blue collar worker, served on the vestry with a doctor, corporate executives, public officials, and educators. They shared a common vision of a church that was big enough to make all differences less important.

The Very Rev. Dr. James A. Kowalski
Diocese of New York

86 Catholic, without the pope, and with the women; protestant without the gloom.

Catherine Gallouet
Diocese of Rochester

87

We don't have all the answers, and we welcome others who love the questions.

The Rev. Wilifred Allen-Faiella
Diocese of Southeast Florida

88

The Bible says we should make a joyful noise unto the Lord. Laughter is as joyful a noise as you'll ever hear and there's a lot of it in an Episcopal church.

David Hunter
Diocese of East Tennessee

89

I don't know why anyone would become a member of a crazy church like ours, but I am a Christian of a peculiarly sacramental sort because of something that happened when I was thirteen. My parents sent me off to Christ School near Asheville, North Carolina, and on the first Sunday the boys were lined up and marched into chapel, which was quickly filling with smoke (under the direction of a senior named Terry Holmes). Some of the new boys passed out and had to be dragged out onto the lawn to recover, but I stayed, survived, and loved it.

Ormonde Plater
Diocese of Louisiana

Episcopalians don't tend to be demonstrative,
no one expects you to shout Amen or hallelu-
jah! On the other hand, it's OK if you do.

Donna H. Barthle
Diocese of Central Pennsylvania

I love the fact that I can have stimulating conversation in class and disagree with the priest, or even the Bishop, and not get kicked because it is all right to use your mind and not be a rubber stamp for anyone. Christ died to save us from our sins, not our minds.

Pat Fortenberry
Diocese of East Tennessee

92

Many whom we know well are starved for the spiritual food we receive daily.

Louie Crew
Diocese of Newark

93

However you like to worship, there are
Episcopalians who like doing it that way too.

Andrew Wetmore
Diocese of Rhode Island

94

Ours is the perfect church for people who aren't perfect.

John F. Schwaller
Diocese of Minnesota

95

I'm comforted by the fact that I am part of a church that allows for differing viewpoints and open debate. While many label our church as "wishy-washy" or divided on the issues, I think that my faith is stronger for my being an active participant in trying to understand God's will. When I hear or read the spirited opinions of my fellow Episcopalians, I find that I am grateful to them, whether I agree with their viewpoints or not. They are contributing to the vitality of our church, and keeping us all honest.

Jennifer Hanshaw Hackett
Diocese of Bethlehem

Our church service is called a 'Celebration,'
and most of the time we do.

Linda Strohmier
Diocese of New Jersey

97

Where a woman's place is in the House of Bishops.

98

We change and transform lives in Christ.

Amada Demers
Diocese of Texas

Our Eucharistic table is not made less special if all are invited, which is contrary to the understanding that I grew up with. Adjusting to the idea that everyone is invited to this most holy meal took me some time, but it has become one of the things I love most about the Church. Understanding that the true presence in the body of Christ is strong enough to survive inside someone who might seem less worthy requires more, not less, faith in its power. I am saddened that I cannot share in communion at my parents' church, and that they will not receive in mine, but I would rather be in that position than the other way around.

Sean P. Hackett
Diocese of Bethlehem

100

There's no such thing as a politically incorrect Episcopalian. There are conservative Episcopalians and liberal Episcopalians. There are straight Episcopalians and LBGT Episcopalians. There are Catholics and Protestants. There are African, English, Asian, and Alaskan Episcopalians. And none of the above. The Episcopal Church doesn't offer you set dogma or pat answers, or a list of do's and don'ts. There's room for all kinds of people and all kinds of theologies. What the Episcopal Church does offer you is a way of prayer, a way of thinking and asking questions, a way of life in this often confusing, conflicting, and complicated world, a way that may lead you closer to God.

Jacqueline Schmitt
Diocese of Chicago

101

Out of habit Episcopalians don't change any-
thing easily, so they can form ironclad habits.
They never stop to compare what others
believe or do, but settle comfortably into the
habit of being Episcopalian. The thing is that
such a habit, followed year after year,
immerses us in the biblical language of the
Book of Common Prayer and in the story of
Jesus—to say nothing of making a life-giving
habit of the weekly Eucharist. Such habits
make life pretty special.

Loren B. Mead
Diocese of Washington